i or h

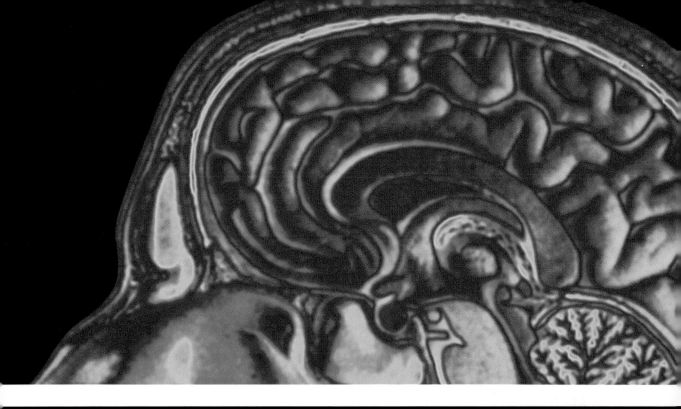

CUTTING EDGE MEDICINE

Seeing Inside the Body

Andrew Solway

W

FRANKLIN WATTS

LONDON•SYDNEY

First published in 2007 by
Franklin Watts
338 Euston Road
London NW1 3BH

Franklin Watts Australia
Hachette Children's Books
Level 17/207 Kent St, Sydney, NSW 2000

Produced by Arcturus Publishing Limited
26/27 Bickels Yard, 151–153 Bermondsey Street
London SE1 3HA

Editor: Alex Woolf
Designer: Nick Phipps
Consultant: Dr Eleanor Clarke

Picture credits:
Science Photo Library: 5 (Mehau Kulyk), 7 (Andrew Lambert Photography), 9, 10, 13
(Gusto), 15 (Mauro Fermariello), 16 (Sovereign, ISM), 19 (Dr M.O. Habert, Pitié-Salpatiere,
ISM), 20 (Wellcome Dept. of Cognitive Neurology), 22 (CC Studio), cover and 25 (Alfred
Pasieka), 26 (Simon Fraser), 29 (Arthur Toga/UCLA), 31 (Victor Habbick Visions), 33 (Saturn
Stills), 34 (Dr Najeeb Layyous), 36 (CNRI), 39 (Zephyr), 40 (David M. Martin, MD),
43 (Princess Margaret Rose Orthopaedic Hospital), 44 (James King-Holmes), 47 (ISM),
48 (Sovereign, ISM), 51 (Sam Ogden), 53 (MIT AI Lab/Surgical Planning Lab/Brigham &
Women's Hospital), 55 (University of Durham/Simon Fraser), 57 (David Parker),
58 (Erik Viktor).

Every attempt has been made to clear copyright. Should there be any inadvertent omission,
please apply to the publisher for rectification.

A CIP catalogue record for this book is available from the British Library.

Dewey Decimal Classification Number: 618.1' 780599

ISBN: 978 0 7496 6974 4

Printed in China

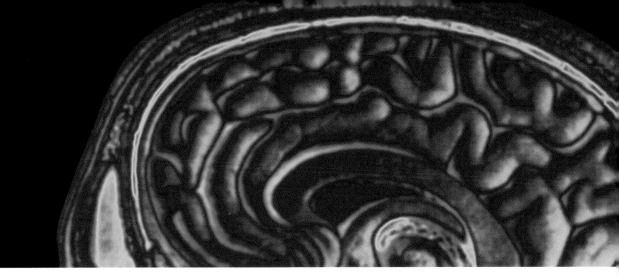

Contents

CHAPTER 1

What is Medical Imaging?

On 1 October 1971, a small hospital in London tested out a strange-looking machine. It was a large, gleaming white box structure with a circular hole in it, big enough for a patient's head. A woman was lying in front of the machine, with her head in the hole. As the machine hummed and whirred, an anxious group of people watched a TV screen close by. After several minutes a black and white picture formed, showing a cross-section through the patient's brain. The watchers pointed excitedly at the screen and began to clap and cheer.

CUTTING EDGE SCIENCE

Why do we need to see inside the body?

One of the most challenging parts of a doctor's job is the diagnosis of a patient's illness. Diagnosis is the process of finding out what is wrong with a patient. Before the development of X-rays and medical imaging, doctors had just two main ways of reaching a diagnosis. They could ask their patients to describe their symptoms, and they could carry out a clinical examination – observing, feeling and listening to the patient's body in order to discover the problem.

These methods remain very important, but they are not always reliable because the body is highly complex and the symptoms of illnesses are often similar. The ability to see inside the body has equipped doctors with a third method of diagnosing illnesses – one that can pinpoint the source and location of a problem with an accuracy that was not previously possible. As we shall discover in this book, medical imaging has transformed medicine and greatly improved the treatment of illnesses such as cancer, stroke, epilepsy, multiple sclerosis and many others.

The first scanner

What was happening? This was the first hospital test of the CT scanner – a machine that used X-rays (see page 7) to scan parts of the body and to form pictures of what was inside. The CT scanner was the first of several different kinds of scanner that have revolutionized medicine since the 1970s. Using scanners to make pictures of the inside of the body is known as medical imaging. To learn more about CT scanners, see Chapter 3.

The first medical test of a scanner was a great success. The images taken by the CT scanner showed a dark, circular shape in the front part of the brain – they indicated the location of an abnormal sac containing fluid, called a cyst. The patient had an operation to remove the cyst. After the operation, the surgeon said that the cyst looked 'exactly like the picture!'

Tools for diagnosis

Medical imaging has given doctors a set of powerful new tools for diagnosing a patient's problems. Modern scanners can create excellent pictures of the body's internal organs (parts such as the liver, lungs and heart). Some scanners can create 3-D pictures, while others can highlight a particular type of problem, such as a tumour (an abnormal growth or mass of cells). However, the story of scanners really began in the late 19th century, with the discovery of X-rays.

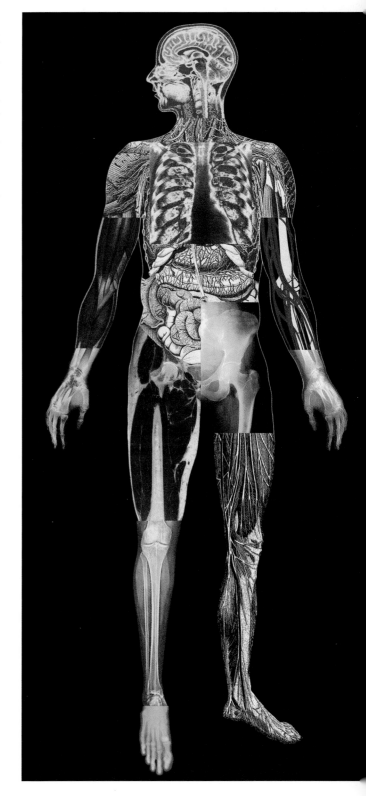

This image of the human body was made using several types of imaging, including an MRI scan (the head) and an X-ray (the pelvis).

CHAPTER 2

X-rays

In November 1895, a German physics professor called Wilhelm Röntgen was experimenting in his laboratory with a cathode ray tube. This was a glass tube with all the air pumped out of it, which contained two wires connected to a powerful battery.

Röntgen was using the cathode ray tube in the dark. He noticed that a screen covered with fluorescent material some distance from the tube was shining brightly. (A fluorescent material glows when light or some other kind of energy hits it.) Röntgen knew that the shining could not be produced by cathode rays (see panel), because these rays cannot travel more than a few centimetres through air. He realized that the cathode ray tube was producing some other kind of radiation. Radiation is a kind of energy that travels in the form of waves or rays. Röntgen called this new radiation 'X-rays'.

An accidental discovery

Röntgen tried to find out more about the new rays. He held up various materials between the cathode ray tube and the fluorescent

CUTTING EDGE   SCIENCE

Cathode ray tubes
Scientists experimenting with electricity tried pumping all the air out of a glass tube in order to see whether electricity could travel through the vacuum (empty space) inside the tube. They found that when the electricity passed through a vacuum, it produced 'cathode rays', which travelled in a straight line from the cathode (negative end) of the tube to the anode (the positive end). Today, cathode ray tubes are used in television sets and computer monitors.

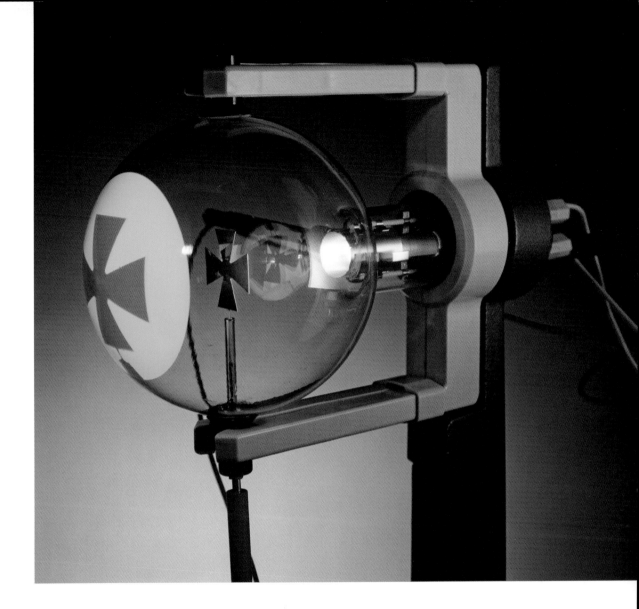

screen, to see if the rays went through them or not. At some point during his experiments, Röntgen accidentally put his hand in front of the screen. The soft parts of his hand hardly showed on the screen, but the X-rays did not pass through his bones, which showed on the screen as dark 'shadows'. Röntgen had made the first X-ray image.

In a cathode ray tube, the cathode rays cause the tube to glow when they hit the glass. In this tube, a cross, hung between the cathode and the anode, blocks some of the cathode rays and produces a shadow on the glass.

What are X-rays?

X-rays are a kind of energy, similar to light. The energy of light and X-rays spreads out from its source in waves, like ripples in a pond. However, light waves and X-rays are pure energy, and can travel much further than waves in water. Light and X-rays are just part of a whole range of different types of radiation, which together make up the electromagnetic spectrum. At one end of the spectrum are low-energy waves like radio waves, while light waves are somewhere in the middle. X-rays are very high-energy waves.

Because of their high energy, X-rays can pass through many materials that light cannot pass through. However, bones are thick and dense enough to block X-rays. In a medical X-ray, X-rays are shone through the body onto photographic film. The X-rays cannot pass through the patient's bones, so the bones form 'shadows' on the film. Depending on how the film is developed, the bones may show up as dark against a light background, or light against a dark background. Today, most radiology departments in hospitals and clinics no longer use photographic film for X-rays, but have switched to digital technology (see page 13).

CUTTING EDGE   SCIENTISTS

Wilhelm Röntgen (1845–1923)

Wilhelm Röntgen was born in Lennep, Germany, but when he was three his family moved to the Netherlands. At school, Röntgen was not obviously bright, although he loved natural history and spent much time roaming the countryside. He was also very good at making machines. In 1869 he received his PhD in physics from the University of Utrecht in the Netherlands. Röntgen was a lecturer and later a professor at several universities before he moved to Würtzburg, Germany, where he made his X-ray discoveries. In 1901 he was awarded the first Nobel Prize in Physics for his work on X-rays.

Spreading like wildfire

Röntgen discovered that the X-rays caused photographic film to blacken, and he made use of this property to create the first X-ray pictures. Röntgen's paper on X-rays was published at the end of December 1895. Newspapers and magazines quickly picked up the sensational story. Many scientists were experimenting with cathode ray tubes similar to Röntgen's, and within weeks they were producing X-ray pictures. Doctors immediately saw how useful X-rays could be in their own profession. In February 1896, less than two months after Röntgen's discovery was made public, Edwin Frost, a doctor in Dartmouth College in New Hampshire,

USA, produced an X-ray picture that was used to diagnose a broken wrist.

The first X-rays were pictures taken on photographic film, but by March 1896 the famous inventor Thomas Edison had developed an instrument called a fluoroscope, which showed X-ray pictures in real time as moving images on a fluorescent screen. Investigating the body using moving real-time X-ray pictures is called fluoroscopy.

At first, X-rays could only make a person's bones visible. Later, in the 1920s, researchers found that by injecting special dyes into a person's bloodstream, they could also make blood vessels show up on an X-ray. This use of X-rays became known as angiography (see pages 12–13 and 36–37).

Dangerous rays

High-energy radiation like X-rays can be harmful. Several hours' exposure to X-rays can cause injuries, such as skin burns and hair loss. This can occur within a few hours or days. With exposure to smaller doses of X-rays over a longer period, the damage is slower

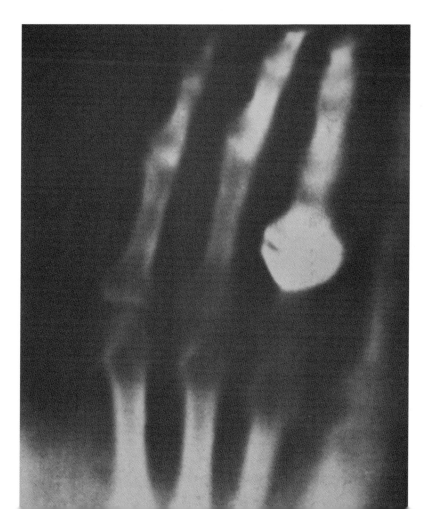

Röntgen's scientific paper included this X-ray picture of his wife's hand. It was one of the first X-rays ever taken. You can see the bones of Anna Röntgen's hand and the ring on her finger.

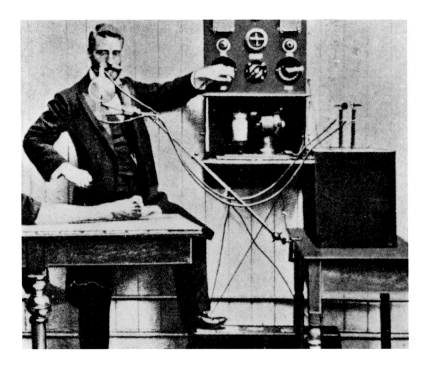

This early, portable X-ray machine was designed for military use. The man using it, Ernest Harnack, worked at the London Hospital in the UK. Like Clarence Dally, Harnack suffered injuries from X-ray exposure, and eventually died of cancer.

to show. It can take several years to appear, and it often shows as cancer.

The dangers of X-rays were not immediately recognized, and they were used in many ways that were unsafe. The physicist Nikolai Tesla warned experimenters in 1896 that they 'should not get too close to the X-ray tube', but his warning was often ignored. In 1904, Clarence Dally, Thomas Edison's chief X-ray researcher, died from cancers caused by excessive exposure to X-rays. Many other early researchers also became ill or died because of damage caused by X-rays. Radiologists (people who take X-ray photographs) began to wear protective clothing and to limit their exposure to X-rays.

The X-ray craze

Although the injuries and illnesses of X-ray researchers and patients showed that X-rays could be dangerous, this did not stop the widespread use of X-ray machines, sometimes for trivial purposes. In the USA there were X-ray slot machines in some cities, which invited people to look at the bones of their hands. As late as the 1940s there were 'Foot-o-Scope' machines in shoe shops that showed the bones of customers' feet.

Improvements in X-rays

Although fluoroscopes showed a picture straight away, early X-ray machines took up to two hours to get a good picture on film. Improvements were made to X-ray machines in the early twentieth century, and by 1906 the required exposure time was no more than a few seconds, greatly reducing the amount of radiation absorbed by the person being X-rayed, making them much safer.

Other improvements produced much clearer, brighter X-ray pictures. In 1913 the German doctor Gustav Bucky found that he could get rid of most 'stray' X-rays, which caused blurring and 'snow' on X-ray pictures, by putting metal grids in front of the X-ray tube and between the patient and the plate. An American inventor, Hollis Potter, improved this grid by moving the grids slowly while the X-ray picture was being taken. The grids still improved the image, but the shadow of the grid did not appear on the final picture.

Safety regulations

Although X-rays no longer caused burns, prolonged exposure to the rays could still lead to problems such as cancer later in life. The long-term effects of X-rays only gradually became clear, but by the 1930s scientists had plenty of evidence that X-rays could be harmful in high doses. In 1931 a maximum X-ray dosage limit was introduced, beyond which it was thought the X-rays could be harmful.

The German physicist Otto Glasser developed a method for measuring radiation exposure that made it safer for those who

CUTTING EDGE   MOMENTS

X-rays in court

Almost as soon as they were discovered, X-rays proved to be useful in court cases. During Christmas 1895, George Holder shot fellow Canadian Tolman Cunnings in the leg in a Montreal bar. Doctors could not find the bullet. In 1896 Cunnings took Holder to court. Holder's lawyers said that Holder had not shot Cunnings and there was no bullet to prove that he had. Cunnings then had his leg X-rayed and the resulting image showed the bullet lodged there. Doctors removed the bullet, and this together with the X-ray picture were enough to convict Holder.

worked with radiation equipment. Workers wore a badge made of photographic film that went black if they were exposed to too much X-ray radiation. Radiologists (X-ray specialists) still wear a similar type of detector today.

Development of X-rays

By 1905 X-rays were being widely used as a medical tool. They were used to look at bones where there was a suspected fracture (break). Chest X-rays could be used to identify pneumonia, lung cancer and oedema (fluid in the lungs).

The X-ray fluoroscope was useful for on-the-spot examinations, but for good-quality images and a permanent record, an X-ray picture was best. Taking large numbers of X-ray pictures was slow work until 1946, when George Schoenander developed an automatic film cassette that could take X-ray pictures at a rate of 1.5 per second. By 1953 the film cassette could take 6 pictures per second.

CUTTING EDGE   FACTS

The pros and cons of X-rays

The main advantages of X-rays are their widespread availability and relative cheapness compared to other kinds of scan. Also, it is possible to take many X-ray images per second to show a 'movie' of the area of interest. Their main disadvantages are the fact that they do not show most of the body's soft tissues (its muscles and organs, for example), and they only show a 2-D (flat) view, usually in black and white (although X-rays can be artificially coloured).

X-ray TV

As X-ray machines improved, it became possible to obtain a good image using much smaller doses of X-rays. In 1955 another invention called the image intensifier made it possible to use smaller doses of X-rays when using a fluoroscope. The image intensifier amplified (made stronger and clearer) the fluoroscope images. The amplified images could be displayed on a TV screen. By the 1960s this 'X-ray TV' had replaced the fluoroscope.

With an image intensifier, angiography (the injecting of dyes into a patient's bloodstream to make the blood vessels show up on an

X-ray) became a much more useful tool. Angiography can be used to find problems with blood flow in any part of the body, including the heart.

Digital X-rays

Until quite recently, all X-ray pictures were produced by shining X-rays onto photographic film. This changed in 2000, when digital X-ray machines became available. Digital X-ray images are coded as a series of numbers. To make a digital X-ray picture, X-rays are shone through the body onto an array of thousands of digital detectors. Each detector measures the amount of X-rays that falls upon it as a number. All the numbers together make a digital image, which is stored on a computer.

Digital X-rays have many advantages over traditional X-rays. Doctors can choose to view them on screen or as a printout, and they can send them in just a few seconds to colleagues in different hospitals. Digital images can easily be altered to make them clearer. And they can be stored on CD as a permanent record when the patient is discharged from care.

Two modern X-ray machines. Compared to the early machine shown on page 10, modern machines are far quicker and produce better images, using only a fiftieth of the X-rays.

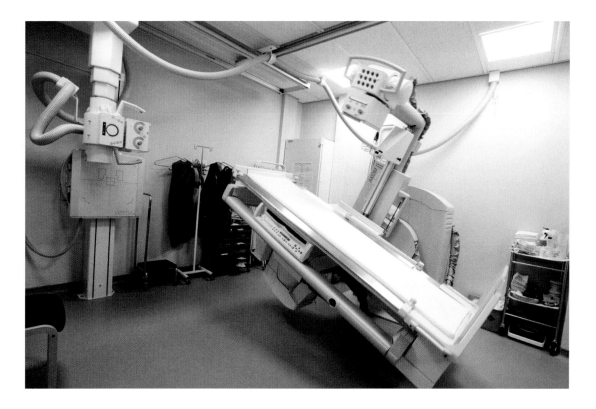

CHAPTER 3

Adding in Computers

Bones and teeth show up on X-ray pictures because they absorb X-rays (they do not allow them to pass through). By contrast, the body's soft tissues hardly show up on X-ray pictures because most X-rays pass through them. The soft tissues are not completely transparent, however. You can see a 'ghost' image of the soft areas on the X-ray. This is because the soft tissues absorb a small amount of X-rays as they pass through the body. In the 1960s, scientists worked on ways of using this partial absorption by the soft tissues to produce much more complete images of the inside of the body.

The computed tomography (CT) scanner

In 1967, English engineer Godfrey Hounsfield had the idea of building a machine to make better images of the soft tissues of the body by taking X-ray photographs of the body at different angles. The soft tissues would absorb more X-rays or less, depending on their depth at the particular angle the photograph was taken. A computer could then be used to build these pictures into a view of a slice through the body. This would give a sense of the depth and position of internal structures, including its soft tissues, that would never be possible with a conventional X-ray.

CUTTING EDGE   **SCIENCE**

How CT works

In a normal X-ray, the rays from an X-ray tube go through the patient and fall on a piece of photographic film or a fluorescent screen. In a CT scanner, the X-ray tube is set on the inside of a ring structure, opposite an array of sensitive detectors. The person being scanned lies in the centre of the ring. The X-ray tube and the detectors move in a circle around the body, taking many X-ray photographs as they go. They pick up X-rays that have passed through the body at a whole range of different angles. A computer combines the different photographs to create a picture of a slice through the body.

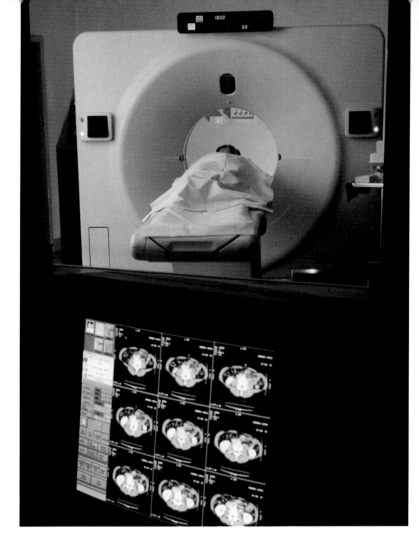

A patient being scanned in a CT machine. On the monitor in the foreground are pictures of some of the body 'slices' taken by the scanner.

Hounsfield called his machine a computed tomography (CT) scanner. The word computed refers to the fact that the machine used a computer to help create its images. The word tomography comes from a Greek word meaning 'slice', and refers to the fact that the CT scanner made images of 'slices' through the body. The CT scanner made its images using a moving X-ray tube, a group of detectors and a computer (see panel).

The first CT scanners were used only for brain scans, but by 1976 larger scanners had been developed that could scan the whole body. The first scanner that Hounsfield built took several hours to collect the information needed for a single 'slice', and it took days for a computer to construct an image. However, by the time the first scanners were used in hospitals, they could produce an image of a single slice in about 4 minutes. Today, CT scanners take 4 to 5 seconds to produce an image, and faster scanners are being developed.

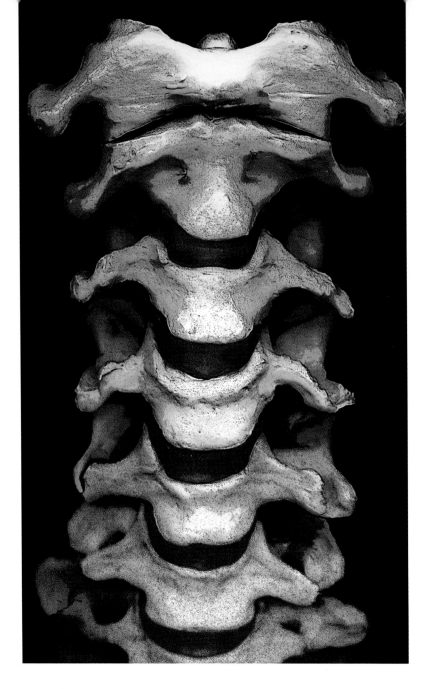

This picture of the bones of the neck looks like a model, but in fact it is a 3-D CT scan. The white areas are bone, while the reddish sections are discs or pads of cartilage (springy tissue between the vertebrae).

Uses for CT

It quickly became clear that CT scanners could see inside the body far more clearly than ordinary X-rays. The first CT machines were used to scan the brain to try to pinpoint the position of a cancer tumour (an abnormal growth of cells or tissues) before an operation to remove it. As they have improved, CT scanners have been used to help diagnose many other problems. They are used to find cancer tumours in other parts of the body, especially in the lungs, liver and intestines. CT scans are also useful for revealing the damage caused by head injuries and for detecting bleeding in the brain. CT is the best technique for diagnosing problems in the chest and lungs because it gives better images of these areas than any other technique.

CT improvements

CT scanners have improved in many ways since the 1970s. The machines have become faster, they give more detail and require smaller doses of X-rays to make images. Faster computers and improved software mean that scanners can produce much better images more quickly. In the 1970s a CT scanner could produce a black-and-white image of a single body 'slice' in about four minutes. Today the latest scanners can produce a much more detailed image in just half a second. Computers can also be programmed to colour the images, to make blood vessels or other details stand out more clearly.

3-D images

The most important advance in CT scanners is their ability to produce 3-D images of different parts of the body on a computer screen. The computer takes the 2-D 'slices' and puts them together to make a three-dimensional model of the region being scanned. A model of this type can be used in many different ways. A radiologist can strip away the skin and muscle to show the internal organs, look at slices through the body from many different angles, or highlight particular structures, such as tumours or blood vessels, with bright colours.

CUTTING EDGE   FACTS

Whole-body CT scans

Modern CT scanners can quickly take images of the whole body. This can be useful in the emergency room. Newly arrived patients with serious injuries can be given a whole-body CT scan, enabling doctors to quickly identify major internal injuries.

Some people have begun to have whole-body CT scans simply as a general check on their health. However, a 2004 study showed that 'health check' scans can themselves pose a risk to health. Modern scanners use low X-ray doses, but in a whole-body CT scan, the patient is exposed to quite a large dose of X-rays. A single scan does not do any harm, but having regular whole-body scans significantly increases the patient's risk of getting cancer later in life.

CHAPTER 4

Harnessing Radioactivity

The CT scanner was not actually the first medical scanner to be developed. Other groups of researchers had been trying for years to build up pictures of the body using radiation other than X-rays. One idea involved using materials that are radioactive. A radioactive material is one that naturally gives off radiation. This radiation can be detected with an instrument such as a Geiger counter.

Early radioactive studies

Radioactivity was first discovered in 1896, a year after the discovery of X-rays. Researchers realized quite early on that if they could make radioactive versions of natural substances and inject them into the body, the radioactivity would act as a 'tag' or 'label' that would make it possible to track the substance inside the body.

In the 1930s scientists managed to produce radioactive versions of elements such as oxygen and hydrogen. The radioactive versions of these elements were called radioisotopes. Researchers injected substances 'tagged' with radioisotopes into the body and tracked where the radioactivity went using a Geiger counter or other detector. At this time no one knew if these radioisotopes were safe. The Hungarian physicist George Hevesy felt that the only way to find out was to test the radioisotopes on himself!

SPECT

Early experiments with radioactive tagging were not designed to produce images of the inside of the body. However, in 1963 US medical researchers David Edwards and Roy Kuhl developed a radioactive tagging technique called SPECT (single photon emission computed tomography) that could produce internal images of the

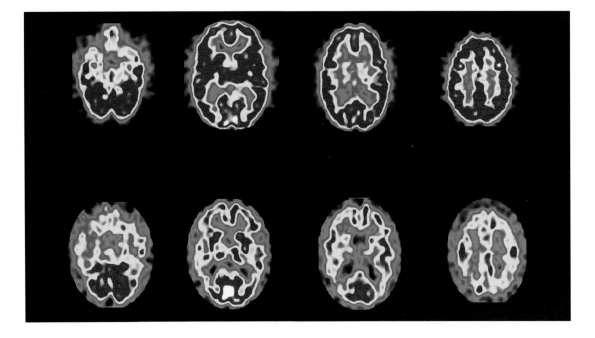

body. A photon is an incredibly small particle of light or other radiation energy, and SPECT produces images by detecting the emission (the sending out) of these photons from the tagged substance. It does this by using cameras sensitive to radiation that rotate around the patient's body.

SPECT does not show images of body structures like an X-ray scan. Rather it shows the distribution of the tagged substance. One substance that is commonly tagged is glucose. Glucose is the 'food' of the body's cells. Cells that are using a lot of energy (usually ones that are growing and dividing) take up a lot of glucose. Cancer cells grow and divide constantly, so a tumour takes up large amounts of glucose. This shows as a concentration of radioactivity on a SPECT scan.

These SPECT scans show several cross-sections through the brain, seen from above. The top row shows a normal brain, and the bottom row shows someone with Alzheimer's disease. Red areas are the most active, while the least active areas are dark blue. There is less activity in the brain of the Alzheimer's sufferer.

CUTTING EDGE FACTS

SPECT
SPECT images are fairly crude, because they do not show body structures, only the distribution of a radioactive substance in the body. However, the scanners are fairly cheap and simple to work, so this type of scan continues to be widely used.

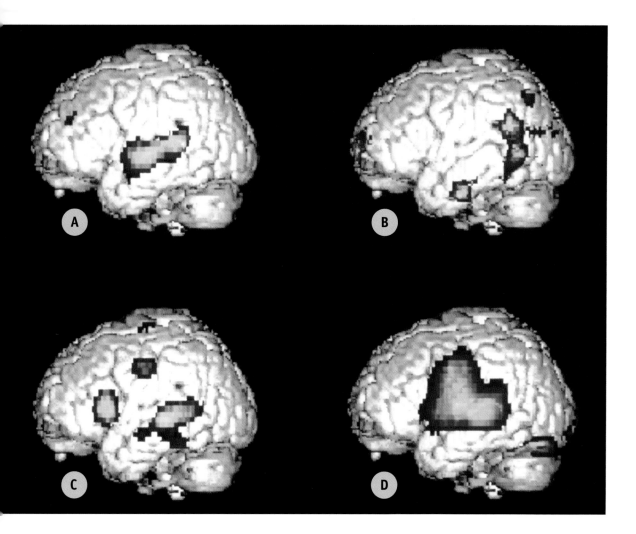

Positron emission tomography

When the CT scanner was launched in 1972, researchers who had been working to improve SPECT scanners saw that a similar technique could be used with radioactive tagging. One team at the the Washington University School of Medicine in St Louis, Missouri, USA, headed by Michel Ter-Pogossian, were working on a device using radioisotopes for imaging the brain. The device looked like a helmet covered in spikes. Ter-Pogossian's team incorporated some ideas from the CT scanner into their own device. The result was a hexagon-shaped machine that surrounded the patient and scanned the body for radioactivity from many different angles. As in CT scanning, a computer then combined the different scans to build up an internal picture of the body.

These PET scans show brain activity when speaking or listening. The orange patches show areas of activity when (A) imagining speech, (B) comprehending what spoken words mean, (C) repeating words, and (D) monitoring speech.

The new technique was given the name positron emission tomography, or PET. It was called this because the radioisotopes used in a PET scanner emit (give off) incredibly small particles called positrons.

Until the 1980s, PET scanners were only used in research, and even today PET is more important in research than in diagnosing illness. This is because PET scanners need very skilled operators to work them, and the radioisotopes that they use have to be made in sophisticated machines that are usually only found in universities and other research facilities. However, PET scans have proved very useful in diagnosing some brain problems (see panel).

How PET works

The radioisotope usually used in PET scans is a type of oxygen that gives off positrons. The patient is given a drink that contains a substance – most commonly glucose – that has been tagged with the radioactive oxygen. Glucose is useful for detecting cancer tumours or other cells that are using a lot of energy (see page 19).

Radioisotopes that give off positrons are different from other radioactive materials because they give off two rays of radiation in exactly opposite directions. If two detectors on opposite sides of the PET scanner pick up a radioactive signal at the same time, this

CUTTING EDGE MOMENTS

Half a brain

In 1985, two-year-old Ryan Peterson was brought to the brain clinic in Los Angeles, California, USA. Ryan had suffered from seizures (fits) since he was born, but they had suddenly started to get worse. Other kinds of scan showed no problems in Ryan's brain, but a PET scan showed that the left half of Ryan's brain was not working properly. In 1986, surgeons removed the entire left half of Ryan's cerebral cortex (the outer part of the brain). Within a year, Ryan was talking and walking, and eventually he was able to go to school. Ryan Peterson's case showed clearly that PET scans can pick up on brain disorders that other scans do not show. Ryan was one of the first people to benefit from a PET scan. Today, PET scans are regularly used to assess the problems of children with epilepsy, although the surgery is usually less drastic.

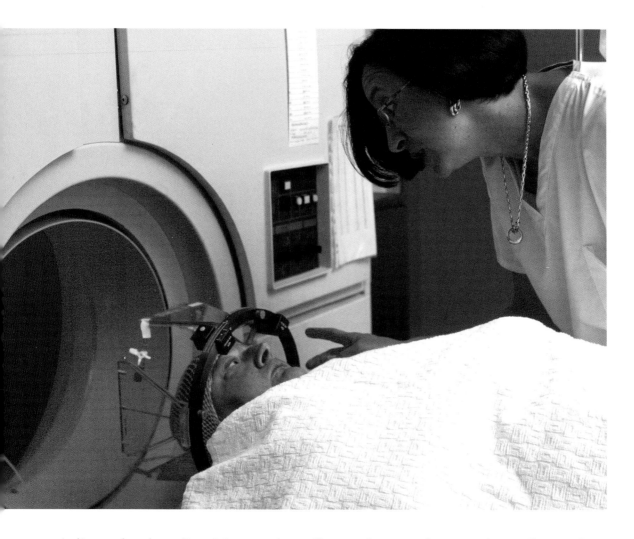

indicates that the radioactivity was given off somewhere on a line between them. From this information a computer can build up an accurate picture of where in the body the tagged glucose is concentrated.

A nurse talks to a patient who is about to undergo a PET scan.

Advantages of PET

Unlike other types of scan, PET focuses on processes that are happening in the body rather than showing structures. For example, if a patient is given tagged glucose, the PET scan will show up cells that are using a lot of energy and dividing rapidly – usually cancer cells. PET is therefore very good at locating tumours.

PET scans can also be used to measure nerve cell activity in the brain, which is useful in the diagnosis of certain brain disorders. If radioactive water is used instead of glucose, the water is absorbed into the blood and shows up in the brain's blood supply. When nerve cells in part of the brain are working hard, blood flow to that part increases to bring the nerve cells more energy in the form of glucose. A PET scan that shows up blood flow is therefore also showing nerve cell activity in different parts of the brain.

This kind of PET scan can be used to diagnose illnesses such as stroke and epilepsy that can cause damage to the brain. For example, brain areas that have been badly damaged by a stroke have no nerve cell activity and so show up as black spots on the PET scan. Epilepsy can have similar symptoms to stroke, but the two illnesses cause different types of damage to the brain. A PET scan can pick up these differences, and so distinguish between stroke victims and people with epilepsy.

Different tracers

Glucose is the most common tracer (substance tagged with radioactivity) used in PET. However, other kinds of tracer can be used to give different kinds of information. For example, a substance called acetate can be tagged with radioactive carbon and used in PET scans of the heart. The muscular tissues of the heart use a different 'fuel' from other cells, and the amount of acetate taken up by the heart muscles is an indicator of how much energy they are using. PET scans using acetate can therefore show up heart problems, for example areas of muscle that are not working properly.

CUTTING EDGE   FACTS

Problems with PET

The radioisotopes that are used for PET only last a short time, so they have to be made at or close to the place where they are used. Making radioisotopes involves using a complex, expensive machine known as a cyclotron. Consequently, PET scanners can only be set up in a limited number of places.

Another disadvantage of PET scans is that they use radioactive materials. The idea of taking a radioactive drink can make some patients anxious. Also, although they are safe for most patients, pregnant mothers cannot have PET scans because the developing baby is especially sensitive to radioactivity and there is a small chance that it could be harmed.

CHAPTER 5

Magnetic Resonance Imaging

Magnetic resonance imaging, or MRI, uses a combination of magnets and radio waves (the kind of waves that carry radio and TV broadcasts) to obtain information about the inside of the body. While CT and X-rays give the best images of bones and other dense tissue, MRI can produce excellent images of any part of the body that contains water. The soft tissues of the body are full of water and show up very well on MRI scans.

Nuclear magnetic resonance

MRI developed out of a technique called NMR (nuclear magnetic resonance), which was developed in the 1950s. NMR was first used by chemists for analysing chemical compounds (finding out what atoms chemicals are made from). NMR uses a combination of magnets and radio waves to identify the different kinds of atom in a compound.

In the 1960s, researchers found that they could also use NMR to look at living tissues. Then, in 1970, US medical researcher Raymond Damadian, who worked at the State University of New York in Brooklyn, began using NMR to investigate tumour cells. He found that cancer tissues produced different NMR signals from healthy

CUTTING EDGE — SCIENCE

How MRI works

MRI scanners work by detecting hydrogen atoms in the body. Hydrogen is a component of water, and since virtually all substances found in the human body contain water, there is not much that the MRI scanners cannot 'see'. One of the few parts that MRI does not pick up are the bones, as these are made mostly of calcium, with little water. MRI scanners direct a combination of magnets and radio waves at the patient's body, causing the body's hydrogen atoms to send out very weak magnetic signals. Detectors in the MRI machine pick up these signals. Hydrogen atoms in different parts of the body give off very slightly different signals, depending on what other atoms are around them. From the differences in the signals, a computer connected to the MRI machine can build up an image of the body and the different tissues in it.

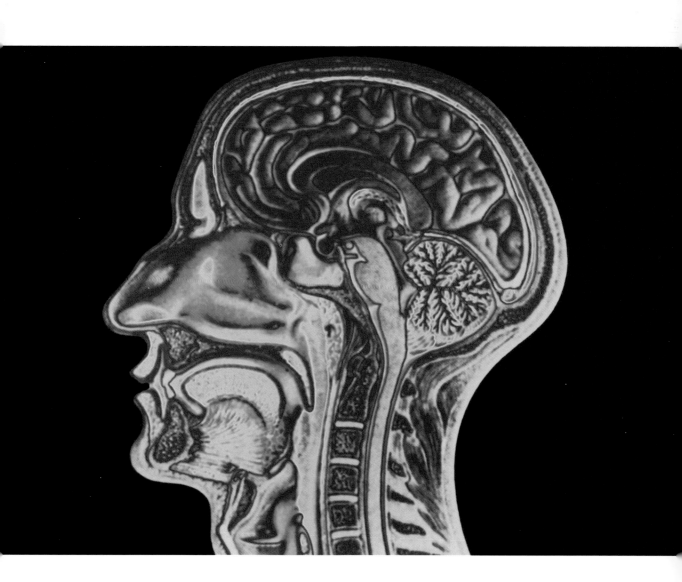

tissues. Damadian began to work on a human-sized NMR machine that could be used to find cancer tumours in the body. He eventually unveiled his machine in 1977.

Although Damadian's machine was impressive, it was not yet an MRI scanner. The images it produced were very crude. The efforts of many other scientists were necessary before an MRI scanner was built that could compete with computed tomography. One of the most important contributions came from the US chemist Paul Lauterbur, who showed how the information from an NMR machine could be manipulated mathematically to turn it into an image. By the early 1980s, ideas from many different people had been put together to make the first practical MRI scanners.

As can be seen from this image of the head, MRI scans give clear and detailed images of the structures of the body. The spine and spinal cord, the brain structures, the space behind the nose, the tongue and the throat are all clearly visible in this scan.

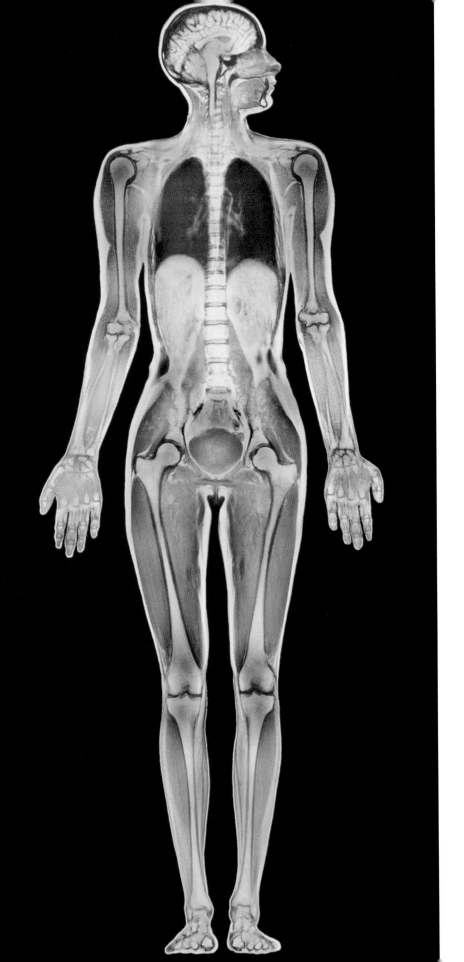

MRI scans were first used for making images of the brain, but they can also be used to make images of many other parts of the body.

Using MRI

By the mid-1980s, MRI scanners were beginning to appear in hospitals. Early MRI scanners could not produce such clear images as CT scanners, the machines were expensive, and it took a long time to obtain a good image. However, there were also advantages to MRI that made doctors keen to use it. Even early MRI scanners produced much better images of soft tissues than were obtainable from CT scanners. MRI scans are especially good for showing soft tissues surrounded by bone or cartilage (tissue similar to bone but springy rather than rigid). In an MRI scan the bones become shadows, while the other tissues are shown in detail.

MRI was particularly useful in diagnosing tumours of the pituitary gland. The pituitary gland is at the base of the brain and is surrounded by the bones of the skull. Only an MRI scan gave clear enough images of the pituitary to show up a tumour in that area.

Another early use of MRI was to diagnose multiple sclerosis (MS). This is a disease in which nerves in the brain and spinal cord become damaged when they lose the protective layer of fatty tissue that surrounds them (called a myelin sheath). The symptoms of MS are very variable, depending on how much damage there is to the nerves. An MRI scan shows clearly this kind of nerve damage, allowing doctors to be sure of the diagnosis and to assess how severe the disease might be.

CUTTING EDGE   SCIENCE

MRI magnets

One important safety measure with MRI is to avoid taking anything magnetic into the scanner room. The magnets used in MRI scanners are immensely powerful. The main magnet can be up to 40,000 times stronger than the Earth's magnetic field. A magnetic object inside the body, such as a pacemaker (an electrical device inserted into the body to stimulate the heart to beat in a normal rhythm) or a clip closing a blood vessel, can be dangerous. There have been a few accidents in which objects as large as oxygen tanks, and even a fork-lift truck, have been dragged across the room by the power of an MRI magnet.

In the early days of MRI, there were some worries that the strong magnetic fields inside the MRI machine might harm patients. However, no harmful effects were found, and MRI is now considered safer than CT and PET, which rely on radiation that can potentially be harmful in large doses.

3-D images

Modern MRI scanners are able to create 3-D images as well as flat 'slices' through the body. These images are made up of small 3-D blocks called voxels. These are similar to the pixels, the tiny dots of light that make up a flat computer image. A 3-D image constructed using voxels can be rotated and 'cut' in any direction. This allows a surgeon planning an operation, for instance, to look at an organ or a tumour from several different angles.

Functional MRI

One newer form of MRI has greatly expanded the ways it can be used in studies of how the brain works. In 1990 the Japanese scientist Seiji Ogawa and colleagues showed that it was possible to use MRI to detect changes in blood flow within the brain. Using MRI in this way is known as functional MRI, or fMRI.

When nerve cells are active they use oxygen. Oxygen is carried to nerve cells in the blood, so a few seconds after nerve cells in a part of the brain become active, the blood flow to that part of the brain increases. Measuring the blood flow within the brain is therefore a fairly accurate guide to brain activity. So, like PET (see pages 20–23), fMRI is a powerful tool for mapping activity in different parts of the brain. The advantage of fMRI over PET is that fMRI machines do not need to be near facilities for

CUTTING EDGE   DEBATES

Does fMRI work?

Since its introduction in the 1990s, fMRI has been used in many studies to support a number of theories. For instance, there have been studies to show how coffee affects the brain, how women react to cartoons and how adverts affect people watching sports events. Many scientists criticize the conclusions drawn from these kinds of studies. They point out that it takes several seconds to produce each fMRI image, but brain activity patterns can change much more rapidly than this. Also, not all scientists agree with the idea that particular parts of the brain have specific jobs – they point to other evidence suggesting that brain functions cannot be localized in this way. Supporters of fMRI argue that these criticisms are problems with particular studies, not with the fMRI technique itself.

producing radioisotopes, and the images they produce are more detailed than PET images.

Scientists have used fMRI scans in many studies of brain activity. The brain of a subject is first scanned while the person is resting to get a 'baseline' picture of brain activity. The subject is then given a simple activity to do, for instance speaking, reading, picking up an object or remembering something. MRI scans are taken during the activity, and the results of the baseline scan are subtracted. The result is a series of images showing the areas of the brain that are most active during the activity.

As with CT scanners, modern MRI scanners can produce 3-D images of the brain and other body structures.

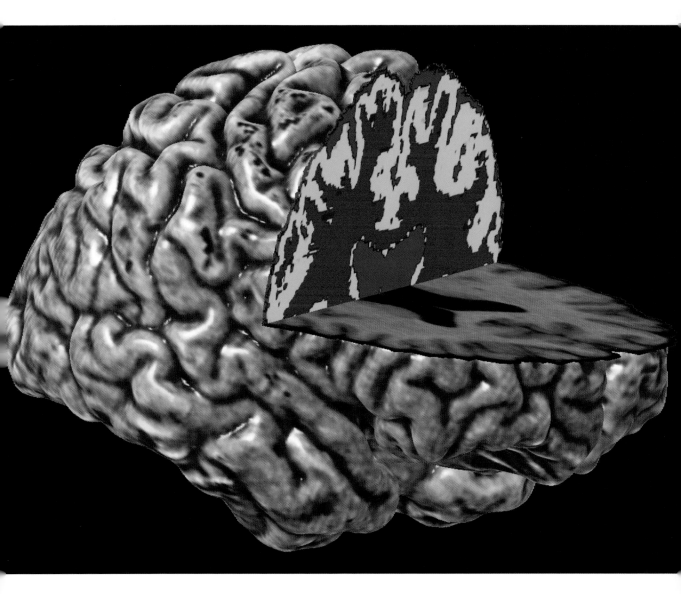

CHAPTER 6

Seeing with Sound

About halfway through her pregnancy, a woman goes to the hospital for a check-up. The check-up is to make sure the fetus is developing properly. As part of the check-up, the midwife does an ultrasound scan to check measurements such as the head diameter. The midwife moves the ultrasound probe over the mother's abdomen. At first all they see on the TV monitor attached to the probe is a blur of white 'snow'. Then, as the midwife finds the right place, they see the shape of the unborn baby curled up inside its mother's uterus (womb).

How ultrasound works

Ultrasound works by sending pulses of very high-pitched sound, far higher than humans can hear, into the body (see panel). Like ordinary sound, ultrasound is made up of vibrations. Some of these vibrations pass straight through the body, but others bounce back from the organs inside the body, like high-pitched echoes. The ultrasound echoes are picked up by detectors inside the ultrasound probe. It is important to get a good contact between the probe and

CUTTING EDGE   SCIENCE

What is ultrasound?

Ultrasound is sound so high-pitched it is beyond human hearing. The sounds are made by special crystals called piezoelectric crystals that vibrate when a rapidly changing electric current (a flow of electricity) is passed through them. The sounds produced in modern ultrasound equipment can be over 300 times higher than the highest sounds we can hear.

the skin – to help do this the probe is coated with a gel. The echoes from many different pulses are processed by a computer, which builds up the information into an image.

The development of ultrasound

Researchers were trying to use sound to look inside the body as early as 1937, when the Austrian brothers Karl and Friedrich Dussik sent sound waves through the skull of a patient with a brain disease. However, the Dussiks' experiments had little success.

The development of ultrasound was helped by the invention of sonar during World War II. Ships used sonar to check the depth of the water and to get a picture of the seabed. The sonar system sent out short sound pulses into the water, which bounced back from the seabed. The echoes were picked up by a special microphone. The time taken for the sound pulses to return gave a measure of the distance from the ship to the seabed, and so the depth of the water.

Another device developed during World War II was the ultrasound flaw detector, which could find hidden cracks within pieces of metal. This was used to check metal structures, such as planes and tanks, for safety, as cracks in a metal weaken it. Many researchers were convinced that something similar to the ultrasound flaw detector could be built to detect structures within the body.

During the 1940s and 1950s, researchers took many different approaches to developing ultrasound. Some were interested in producing detailed images of the inside of the body, while others attempted to use ultrasound to detect breast cancer or other tumours. The person who developed ultrasound for looking at the uterus was a Scottish doctor called Ian Donald (see panel).

Ultrasound for babies

At first, Donald was interested in using ultrasound to detect cysts (fibrous growths) in ovaries. Then, in 1959, he noticed that the head of the growing baby gave clear ultrasound readings, and he began to use ultrasound to measure unborn babies' heads.

By 1966 the first ultrasound scanners were being produced commercially. The images were still poor quality, however. Ultrasound would perhaps not have caught on at all if it had not been for studies in the mid-1950s showing that exposure of babies in the uterus to X-rays could cause leukaemia or other cancers. Ultrasound therefore came to be seen as a safe alternative to X-rays.

At present, ultrasound scans are used mainly to check on the growing fetus (the unborn baby) during pregnancy. The fetus is checked at various stages during its growth. Early in pregnancy a woman may be scanned to see if she is carrying more than one fetus, and to confirm the age of the fetus and therefore when the baby is likely to be born.

Women usually have a second ultrasound scan around halfway through their pregnancy. At this stage the fetus is quite well

CUTTING EDGE MOMENTS

Ultrasound to the rescue

In the 1950s, Ian Donald began to experiment with ultrasound, using modified metal flaw detectors as a way to see inside the body. Most doctors thought Donald's ideas would not work. However, in 1957, he used an ultrasound detector to examine a woman who was thought to have a serious cancer that was too far advanced to operate on. With his machine, Donald found that she had an ovarian cyst – a growth on an ovary (a female reproductive organ) that is fairly easy to remove. The diagnosis probably saved the woman's life. The case convinced many doctors that ultrasound could be a useful tool.

developed and the sonographer doing the scan can check that the baby is healthy and developing normally.

If the scan shows that the baby is smaller or bigger than normal, or if the woman is expecting more than one baby, a further scan may be carried out late in the pregnancy.

Ultrasound is also used as a guide for the doctor during an amniocentesis. This is a procedure in which a doctor uses a needle to take a small sample of the amniotic fluid (the fluid surrounding the fetus in the uterus). Doctors carry out an amniocentesis if they are worried that the fetus might have anaemia (thin blood) or that its lungs are not fully developed. Doctors use the ultrasound images to guide the needle during an amniocentesis procedure, to ensure the safety of the fetus.

A pregnant woman having an ultrasound scan. The probe on the woman's abdomen sends out ultrasound waves and picks up the echoes that return from inside the body. The fetus is clearly visible on the monitor.

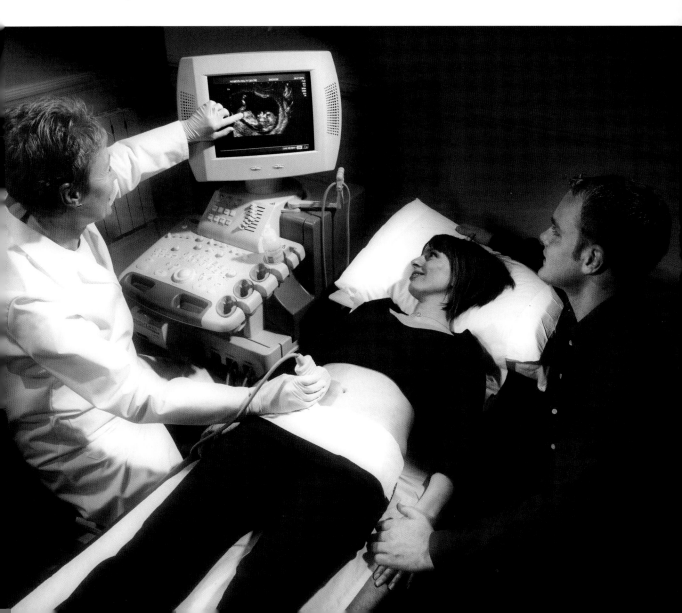

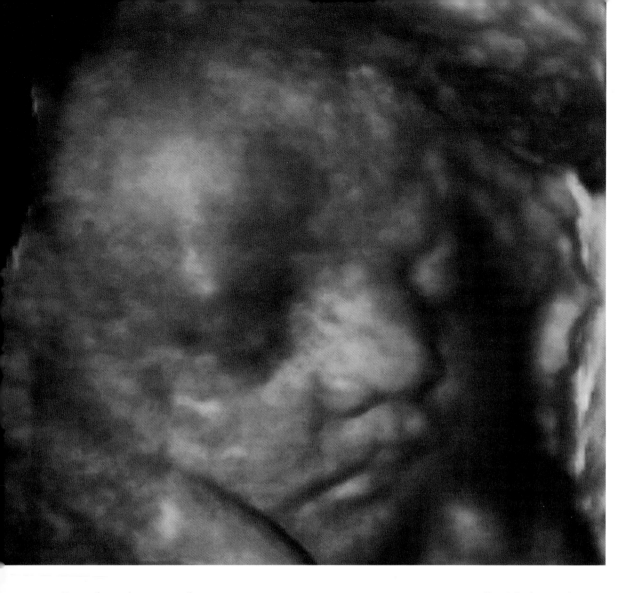

Doppler ultrasound

Another kind of ultrasound, known as Doppler ultrasound, was pioneered in 1955 by two Japanese scientists, Shigeo Satomura and Yasuhara Nimura. Doppler ultrasound uses the Doppler effect to tell whether blood is flowing towards the ultrasound probe or away from it. The Doppler effect is an increase or decrease in the frequency, or pitch, of sound waves, depending on whether they are approaching or moving away from the observer. The Doppler effect is the reason why the siren on an ambulance sounds higher as it approaches you, and lower as it moves away. Doppler ultrasound picks up similar changes in the pitch of echoes coming back to the probe from flowing blood. If the echo is lower in pitch than the original signal, the blood is flowing away from the probe. If it is higher, the blood is flowing towards the probe.

New 3-D ultrasound techniques produce far more detailed images of the fetus than traditional ultrasound can achieve.

During pregnancy, Doppler ultrasound can pick up the heartbeat of a fetus long before it can be heard by other methods, such as using a stethoscope. Doppler ultrasound is also used in general medicine to spot blockages in blood vessels and to diagnose diseases such as arteriosclerosis – a disorder, particularly of old age, in which the walls of the arteries (blood vessels carrying blood from the heart to the rest of the body) thicken and harden. Doppler ultrasound can also be used to diagnose problems with the heart valves (parts that control the flow of blood through the heart).

3-D images

In 2001, ultrasound scanners were developed that could show 3-D images of the fetus in the uterus. The images produced by these scanners were a great improvement on the ultrasound pictures that people had become used to seeing. Ultrasound machines that produce 3-D images are gradually becoming more widespread.

In 2006, researchers in the USA developed a 3-D ultrasound probe just 12 millimetres across. A normal (2-D) ultrasound probe of this size has 64 cables sending information from the probe to the ultrasound machine. The new probe carries 500 cables in a tube of the same diameter. The probe is designed to be fitted on instruments used during laparoscopic (keyhole) surgery. This is surgery carried out using instruments that can be inserted into the body through small incisions (cuts), rather than the large incisions needed for normal surgery. With the new ultrasound probe, surgeons can use 3-D ultrasound images to guide their instruments.

CUTTING EDGE   SCIENCE

Ultrasound treatment

Ultrasound can be used to treat some medical problems rather than just diagnosing them. The vibrations in the tissues, and the warming that this can produce, can be helpful for many joint problems. Ultrasound is also a very effective treatment for kidney and bladder stones. These are hard lumps that sometimes build up in the kidney or bladder, which can be very painful. In a procedure called lithotripsy, ultrasound breaks the stones into small pieces, which are then swept away in the blood or urine.

CHAPTER 7

Following the Traces

Different types of medical imaging are used for different purposes, depending on what the doctor wishes to see. Early X-rays, for instance, showed only bones, and could not be used to look at blood or soft tissues. Then, in 1910, researchers found a way of using X-rays to look at the intestines. They gave the patient a liquid called a contrast medium, which X-rays cannot pass through. The contrast medium coated the intestines, which then showed up clearly on X-rays. In the 1920s scientists found another contrast medium that could be safely injected into the bloodstream. This allowed doctors to take X-ray images of blood vessels in living patients.

In an angiogram, material that is opaque to X-rays (they cannot pass through it) is injected into the blood to make the blood vessels show up. This angiogram shows the blood vessels of the heart.

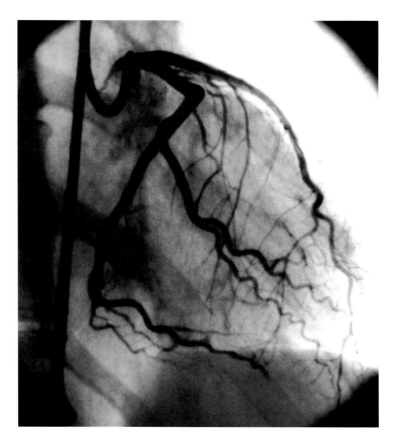

Early experiments

In January 1896, only weeks after Röntgen announced his discovery of X-rays, two Austrian doctors in Vienna took an X-ray picture of the blood vessels in the hand by injecting a compound of the chemical element mercury into the blood vessels of a dead person. This technique could not be used on live patients, however, as mercury is very poisonous.

By 1910, doctors had discovered that they could safely give patients a compound made from the element bismuth to show the intestines on X-rays. Using this technique, doctors were able to find problems such as ulcers and perforations (holes) in the gut lining. Later another element, barium, began to be used instead of bismuth.

In 1921 a French doctor called Jan Sicard accidentally discovered that an oily substance called lipidiol, known to be an effective painkiller, was also an excellent contrast medium. Lipidiol could be used to obtain good X-ray images of the spinal canal (the cavity down the middle of the spine that contains the spinal cord), the uterus, the bladder and some joints. However, it could not be used to X-ray the blood vessels.

X-raying the blood vessels

In the late 1920s, dyes containing the chemical element iodine were tested for use as contrast mediums in the blood. Some of these dyes

CUTTING EDGE   MOMENTS

X-raying the heart

In 1929 a young German hospital doctor, Werner Forssmann, began experimenting with a technique called catheterization. Practising on dead bodies, he worked out a way of inserting a narrow tube called a catheter into a blood vessel and feeding it through the blood vessels to the part of the body to be studied. He then injected a contrast medium into the blood through the catheter and took an X-ray. Forssmann was refused permission to try the experiment on a live patient, but he tried it anyway – on himself. He inserted a catheter 30 centimetres into a vein in his arm and injected contrast medium. Then, with the catheter still in place, he walked downstairs to the X-ray room and took an X-ray picture of the blood vessels in his arm as a document of the experiment. Forssmann was reprimanded for his experiment, but he had proved that the technique was safe. After World War II, other researchers used longer catheters to insert contrast medium into the heart, making X-ray images of the heart possible. In 1956 Forssmann shared the Nobel Prize for Medicine with two other researchers for his pioneering work.

were successful, and it was at last possible to make angiograms (X-rays showing the blood vessels) of living patients. In the late 1920s this technique was adapted for studying blood flow through the heart (see panel).

Contrast mediums for scanners

As with conventional X-rays, the images from CT scanners can be improved by the use of a contrast medium. Contrast mediums containing iodine are used to highlight the blood vessels or the intestines.

A contrast medium is also sometimes useful in MRI scans. Most MRI contrast mediums contain the metal gadolinium. Gadolinium contrast mediums give very clear MRI images of the intestines, the liver and the heart. A contrast medium can also be used for MRI scans of a woman's breast if it is suspected that she has breast cancer. Once it reaches a certain size, a cancer tumour develops its own special blood supply. The contrast medium is injected into the blood and shows up the tumour through this network of extra blood vessels.

Pictures of the lungs

One area of the body that hardly shows up at all in MRI scans is the lungs. This is because the lungs are full of air, which does not have strong magnetic properties. However, a technique developed in the

CUTTING EDGE   SCIENCE

Breast cancer screening

Breast cancer is one of the most common forms of cancer in women. In most developed countries, women over 50 are regularly screened (checked) for signs of breast cancer. Detailed X-rays known as mammograms are usually used for the check. Since the early 1990s, however, researchers have been investigating the possibility of using MRI scans instead. MRI scans are clearer than X-rays and show more detail. However, they take longer and are much more expensive. Also, the extra detail in an MRI scan can occasionally lead to false positives (people being diagnosed with breast cancer when they are perfectly well).

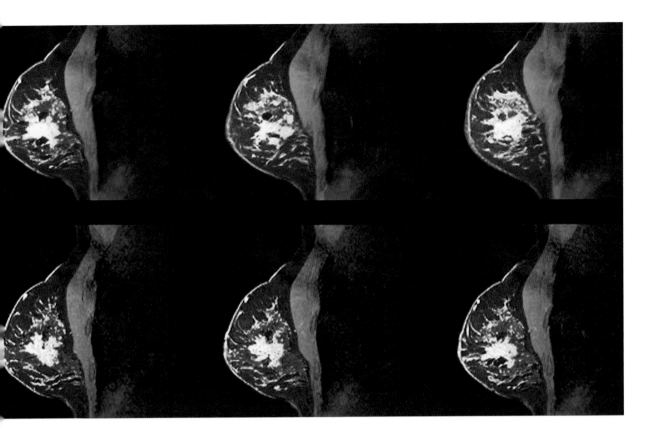

late 1990s by Professor Bill Hersman at the University of New Hampshire, Durham, USA, makes it possible to obtain very clear images of the lungs. In this technique, the patient breathes in a lungful of a special form of either helium or xenon gas. The patient holds the gas in his or her lungs for about ten seconds, during which time MRI scans can be taken. Both of these gases give an MRI signal 100,000 times stronger than that of water, making possible very high-quality images of the lungs. However, the method is currently still in the research stage.

This series of MRI scans shows several cross-sections through a woman's breast. The orange areas show the presence of breast cancer. A gadolinium contrast medium has been used to make the cancer show up clearly.

Computer-enhanced images

The images from a CT or MRI scanner are built up by a computer from a mass of data (information). By instructing the computer to focus on one kind of information and not another, it is possible to tailor a CT or MRI scan to show the information a doctor is interested in. Particular tissues (tumours, for instance) can be coloured brightly, while tissues that are not of interest can be removed from the image.

CHAPTER 8

Long, Thin Cameras

So far, all the techniques we have looked at have involved indirect observation of the inside of the body. X-rays, sound waves and other kinds of radiation all work by detecting the change to a signal directed at or passed into the body, and they then build up an image from that. Since the 1960s, however, there has been another method available to doctors, enabling them to look directly into the body using nothing more complicated than a camera.

This endoscope image of the stomach shows how the walls of the stomach are wrinkled. This allows the stomach to expand when it is filled with food.

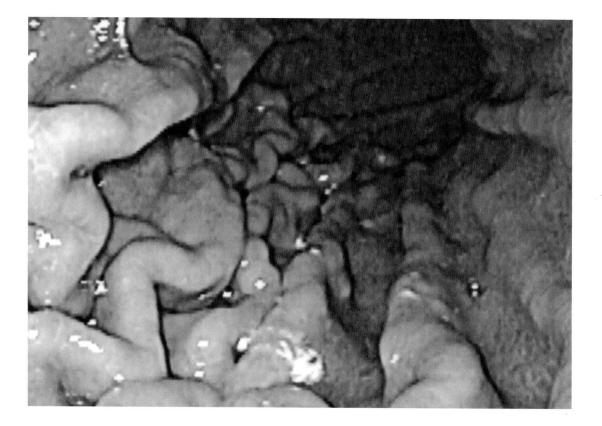

How an endoscope works

The flexible tube of an endoscope is a bundle of optical fibres called a fibre-optic cable. On the end that goes into the body there is a lens to focus light. On the other end are a camera and a lamp. The endoscope is fed into the body through, for example, the mouth, until the end with the lens reaches the part of the body the doctor wishes to look at. Some optical fibres carry light from the lamp down the endoscope to light up the area around the lens. Other fibres carry the image of the area around the lens up the endoscope to the camera. A cable carries the image from the camera to the TV monitor, where the doctor can see it.

The endoscope is a tiny camera at the end of a long, thin, flexible tube. It is inserted into the body through a natural or artificially created opening to allow doctors to look inside the body. The important part of the endoscope is the tube. This is a fibre-optic cable – a bundle of hair-like glass fibres known as optical fibres. Optical fibres can transmit information in the form of pulses of light. They are an important part of today's communications networks, used for carrying telephone calls, the internet, TV and radio programmes to all parts of the world. However, optical fibres were first developed for looking inside the body.

Early endoscopes

Tube-like instruments for looking into the body were first developed in the 19th century – but until the invention of electric light, and bulbs small enough to fit into the body, these devices were not very useful. In 1910, a Swedish doctor, Hans Christian Jacobeus, used a rigid endoscope to look inside the chest, and in 1912 he used a similar instrument to look into the abdomen (stomach area).

Endoscopy took a significant step forward in 1957 when the scientist Basil Hirschowitz and colleagues, working in the USA, developed a flexible endoscope for looking at the stomach, known as a gastroscope. In the course of developing the gastroscope, Hirschowitz's colleague Lawrence Peters produced the first optical fibres. By the mid-1960s, endoscopes were in widespread use.

Using endoscopes

Today, endoscopy is used to diagnose many different medical problems. For example, endoscopes can be fed through the mouth and down the throat to examine the oesophagus (the tube from the throat to the stomach), the stomach and the lower intestine for problems such as bleeding, ulcers (sores in the digestive tract) or inflammation (swelling). An endoscope can be fed through the mouth, down the trachea (windpipe) into the lungs to look for evidence of bronchitis (inflammation of the airways), tumours or infections. All these examinations can be made without making a cut in the body.

For other endoscope examinations, the doctor has to make a small cut to insert the endoscope. A type of endoscope called an arthroscope can be inserted through a small cut to examine the knee or some other joint. An arthroscope is a rigid endoscope with a fairly short tube, because it does not have to be inserted far into the body.

Another kind of endoscope, called a bronchoscope, can be inserted into the chest area through a small cut and used to examine the outside of the lungs and the inside of the chest cavity. This can be helpful to diagnose a problem known as adhesion, in which the chest lining and the outer lining of the lungs become stuck together.

An endoscope can also be used to look at organs in the abdomen such as the intestines, the liver and the gall bladder.

CUTTING EDGE   FACTS

Arthroscopic surgery

Arthroscopic surgery is keyhole surgery of the joints. Until the 1990s, damage to a knee or other joint involved bringing the patient into hospital for several days and making large cuts to get at the joint. Recovery would take weeks or months. With arthroscopic surgery the patient needs to come in only on the day of the operation, and recovery is much quicker.

For an operation on the knee, three tiny cuts are made. The arthroscope is inserted through one cut, and a cannula (a tube carrying salty water) is inserted in the second cut. The water pumped in through the cannula makes the joint swell up, which makes the joint easier to see and gives more space for the operation. The third cut is used for inserting surgical instruments.

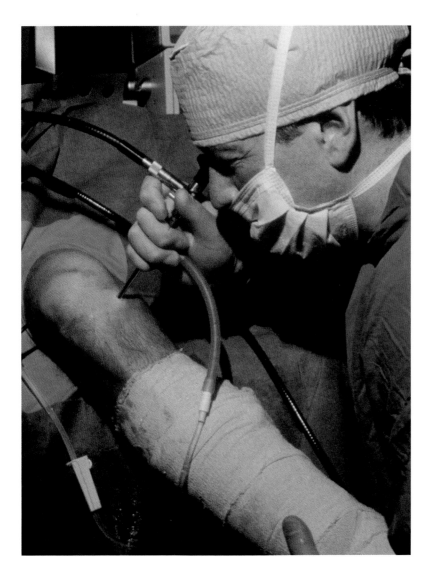

A surgeon uses an arthroscope to examine a patient's knee joint. The arthroscope is a steel tube containing optical fibres, a lens and a light source. Sometimes a scalpel or other surgical tool is attached to allow surgery to be carried out.

Not just for looking

Endoscopes can be used for more than just diagnosing problems. A range of surgical instruments can be fixed to the end of an endoscope and used, for example, to take a biopsy (cut a small sample of tissue for testing).

Endoscopes can also be useful during keyhole surgery. The surgeon inserts specially designed cutting tools or other tiny surgical instruments through small incisions (cuts). Using the endoscope, the surgeon can guide the instruments to the right place and carry out the operation without having to make a large incision in the patient's body.

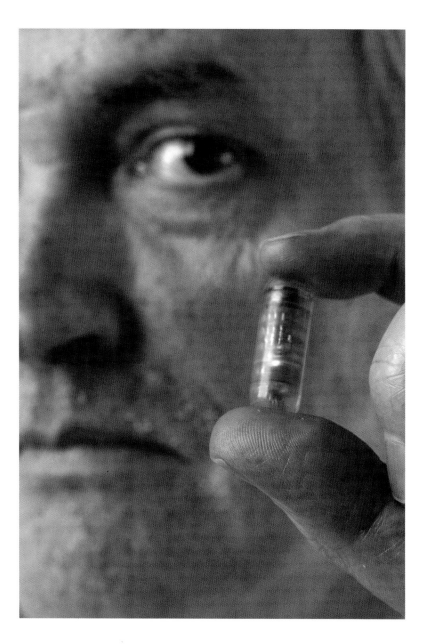

A capsule endoscope, or 'camera in a pill', being held by Professor Paul Swain, who led the team at the Royal London Hospital, UK, that developed the device. Measuring just 11 by 30 millimetres, the capsule endoscope is little bigger than an ordinary pill and has a light source and a radio transmitter. The patient cannot feel the pill once it has been swallowed, and can carry on life as normal. The endoscope is disposable, and is simply flushed down the toilet when the patient passes it.

Camera pill

Ordinary endoscopes can look at the top part of the digestive tract from the throat to just below the stomach, and at the bottom part of the digestive tract (the colon). However, normal endoscopy cannot reach the small intestine, which is between the two.

The wireless capsule endoscope, or the 'camera in a pill', solves this problem. It is a camera small enough to fit into a pill, which the patient swallows. On its journey through the patient's gut, which takes about eight hours, the camera takes up to 50,000 pictures. The images are transmitted to a wireless receiver that the patient wears on his or her belt. The doctor then downloads the images and is able to watch a movie of the camera's trip through the patient's digestive tract.

The camera pill is a good way to diagnose problems such as bleeding in the small intestine, which cannot be diagnosed using other tests.

Robot cameras

Recent research has led to improvements in camera pills to make them even more effective. The newest versions are like tiny robots, which doctors can move about by remote control. These robot cameras can be turned as they move along to look at parts of the intestine wall that the doctor is interested in. They also have tiny clamps that allow them to fix to the wall of the intestine, anchoring the camera in one place so that it does not get swept past an area of interest.

CUTTING EDGE — SCIENCE

Long-distance surgery

In June 2001, 14 patients in a hospital in Rome were examined by a surgeon, who looked at their kidneys through an endoscope. The surgeon then performed a minor kidney operation on some of the patients. Operations of this sort are usually routine, but in this case the surgeon was in Baltimore, Maryland, USA. It was one of the first examples of telesurgery – in which a surgeon operates on a patient from a distance – in this case, from a different continent. Telesurgery uses a combination of video, medical imaging and a remote-controlled robot to carry out the actual surgery. Using a robot in this way is difficult at present, because the surgeon cannot feel what is going on – he can only see and hear the operation. However, researchers are working on software that will allow the surgeon to actually 'feel' what is happening during the operation as well as see it.

CHAPTER 9

Combining Techniques

Each kind of medical imaging has its own strengths and weaknesses. When assessing the pros and cons of different techniques, the key factors are quality, cost, availability and potential for causing harm.

CT scanners give good images quickly, especially for harder tissues. However, CT uses X-rays, which can be harmful to the body in large doses. Because they use X-rays, CT scanners are not used on pregnant women.

PET scans show information about the functioning of tissues (for instance the uptake of glucose) rather than their structure. However, PET uses radioactive materials, which are also dangerous if used too often.

MRI scans are clear and detailed, and fMRI scans can show the processes going on in the body as well as the body's internal structure. MRI does not require dangerous radiation to produce images. However, high-quality MRI scans are slow and expensive to produce. MRI cannot be used on patients who have metal implants or heart pacemakers, and it does not show bones or the lungs. Also, many patients experience feelings of claustrophobia (fear of enclosed spaces) during MRI scans.

Ultrasound is safer than other techniques, which is why it is used during pregnancy. Conventional ultrasound scans are cheaper than other kinds of scan, but they give poor-quality images. Better-quality 3-D ultrasound scans are considerably more expensive.

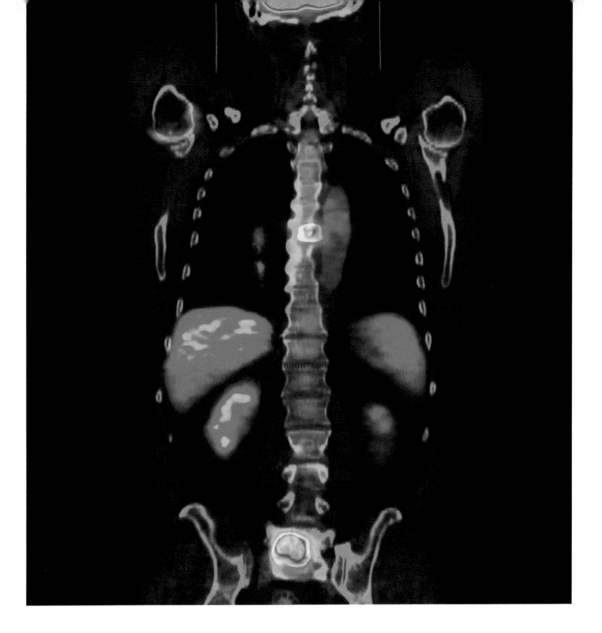

CUTTING EDGE   FACTS

Imaging tumours

One important use of medical imaging is for spotting tumours as early as possible. Early tumours do not show up clearly on CT scans because the cancer tissue does not look different from the tissue around it. A PET scan does show up early tumours because it picks up the faster oxygen uptake of rapidly dividing cancer cells. However, PET scans do not show much structural detail. A combination of a PET scan with a CT scan shows up the early tumours clearly and shows enough structural detail to make it clear where the tumour is located.

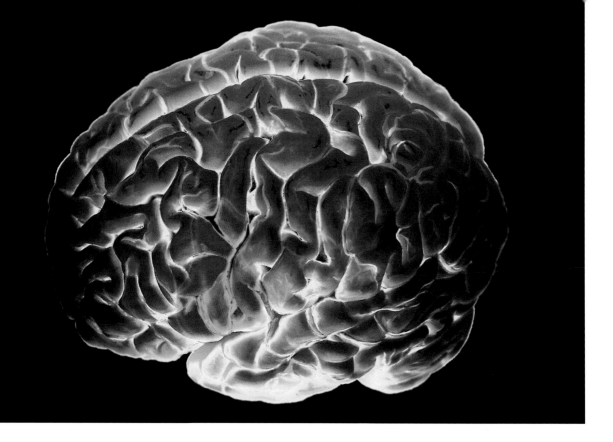

Endoscopy is also a safe technique and it gives good-quality images. However, endoscopes can only look at a small area of the body in each image, and they cannot see through bone or tissue.

In the early 21st century, as the various kinds of scanner have become more widespread, researchers and doctors have begun to combine different imaging techniques. By combining techniques they are able to overcome the weaknesses of particular types of scanner.

This image combines a 3-D MRI scan of the whole brain with a PET scan showing brain activity when the patient is doing a particular task. In this case the scan shows the brain area that is most active when the patient is thinking about specific words.

Improved brain images

Another area where combined scans are useful is for looking at the brain. Normal MRI scans show the structures of the brain in great detail, but they are slow and do not give any information about brain activity. fMRI scans show blood flow in the brain, indicating which parts of the brain are most active. They can also be done several times per second. PET scans are also fast and can show brain activity. Alternatively, PET scans can be tailored to show different types of nerve connections in the brain. A combination of MRI with PET or fMRI scans gives a good picture of the structures of the brain along with information about which parts are active.

At present, combined brain scans are used mainly for brain research. However, they are increasingly being used to show up abnormal activity patterns found in illnesses that affect the brain. Combined MRI/PET scans are also important in research into new drugs (see panel).

Spotting fast changes

One problem with images of the brain is that nerve activity in the brain changes very quickly. An effect may last only a few milliseconds and then disappear or change. Even fMRI and PET cannot keep track of changes that happen at this speed.

Two techniques that can pick up such rapid changes are EEGs (electroencephalograms) and MEGs (magnetoencephalograms). EEGs monitor electrical activity in the brain. In an EEG the doctor places several electrodes (conductors of electricity) on the surface of the head. The electrodes pick up the electrical activity of nerve impulses travelling through the brain. MEGs are similar, but they measure changes in magnetism rather than electrical activity. Both techniques only give a vague idea of where the activity is happening, but they show changes that happen in real time. By combining EEGs and MEGs with brain imaging, researchers can see exactly where moment-by-moment changes are happening.

CUTTING EDGE SCIENCE

PET in drug research

A combination of PET with MRI or CT is proving enormously useful in research into new drugs. Companies developing new drugs have been using PET for some time to test the effects of new drugs on animals. The drug being tested can be radioactively tagged and then PET scans can show where the drug goes in the body.

Now researchers are also using PET, combined with MRI or CT, to test directly the effectiveness of some drugs on humans. For instance, a protein called amyloid forms in the brain in people who have Alzheimer's disease (a disorder that affects the brain, especially late in life). Researchers have found a substance that binds to amyloid in the brain, and this substance can be given a radioactive tag. So the amyloid levels in patients with Alzheimer's can be tested directly using PET. This test is very useful for checking the effectiveness of drugs that treat Alzheimer's by lowering amyloid levels. By doing PET scans before and after administering the drug, any changes in amyloid levels can be measured.

CHAPTER 10

Not Just for Diagnosis

We saw in Chapter 8 that endoscopes can be used in keyhole surgery as well as for diagnosing illness. Today, other kinds of medical imaging are also being used in surgery and to target treatments such as radiation therapy for cancer.

Killing off tumours

Radiation therapy has been used as a treatment for some kinds of cancer for many years. Radiation can be dangerous to humans because it can damage dividing cells. It can also be useful to doctors for the same reason. Cancer cells divide rapidly, so radiation damages cancer cells more than it damages other body tissues. By giving a patient a short, focused dose of gamma rays or X-rays, doctors can sometimes use radiation to kill off tumours. Radiation has been used in this way since the early 20th century.

CUTTING EDGE   MOMENTS

MRI lifts depression

A surprising discovery in 2004 suggests that MRI may have other uses besides imaging. Researchers looking at the brains of depressed patients discovered that after having MRI brain scans, patients with certain kinds of depression were much happier. This improvement in mood lasted for some time. The combination of electrical and magnetic fields produced during MRI scans seem to have worked in some unknown way to lift depression – with no side effects. MRI scans are very expensive, so researchers are now doing animal tests on a smaller, simpler device that produces similar electric and magnetic fields. This kind of magnetic therapy may eventually become a common treatment for depression.

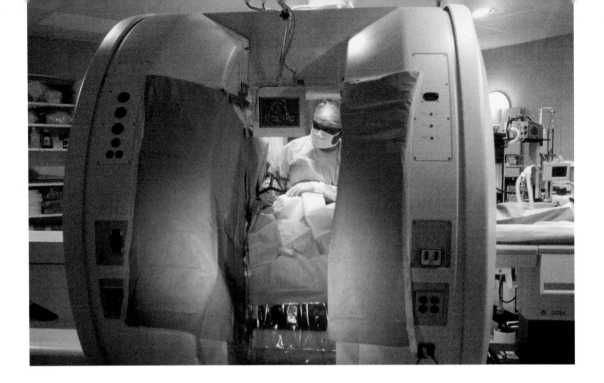

However, radiation therapy can have unpleasant side effects such as hair loss and nausea. Radiation therapy is also not always successful. If the radiation therapy can be more accurately targeted on the cancer tumour, treatment is more likely to be successful and there is less chance of unpleasant side effects. Modern PET, MRI or CT scanners can help to focus radiation very accurately on particular areas of the body. High-quality 3-D images of the cancer tissue enable doctors to see exactly where the radiation needs to be aimed. This makes the therapy more effective and reduces the amount of radiation needed to kill the tumour.

This brain operation is being carried out in the middle of an open-sided MRI scanner. The surgeon uses a 3-D image of the brain (shown on the monitor) to guide his surgery. New scans updating the situation can be taken as the surgery is taking place.

Guiding surgery

Since the late 1990s, advances in MRI scanners and computer software have made it possible for surgeons to perform brain operations that would be almost impossible otherwise. Sometimes brain tumours develop very close to vital parts of the brain. A tiny error by the surgeon could leave the patient paralysed. It is in instances such as these that MRI can help.

Surgeons first take a high-quality, 3-D MRI image of the brain. If the problem is a tumour, the MRI scan is combined with a PET or fMRI image showing the position of the tumour. Another MRI or CT scan could be added to show the position of important blood vessels or other structures that the surgeon needs to see clearly when carrying out the operation.

When the surgeon begins the operation, a TV monitor in the operating theatre shows the MRI image superimposed on a live video of the patient's head. The scan and the real head are exactly aligned using a laser scanner (see panel) and some sophisticated computer software.

Keeping track of the scalpel

As the operation progresses, there may be some movement of tissues within the skull. Consequently, the original MRI image showing the position of the tumour may not be exactly as the surgeon finds it when he or she cuts into the brain. To overcome this problem, the surgeon carries out the whole operation in an advanced MRI scanner that has an open section in the middle where the surgeon can stand. During the operation the surgeon can take additional MRI scans to see if there are any changes in the position of the tumour or other tissues. Because the surgeon is working in an MRI scanner, he or she must use specially designed non-magnetic surgical instruments.

Surgery using MRI imaging is currently used mainly for brain operations. However, the technique could soon be used in other operations, for instance to assist complex operations on bones, the kidneys, the liver and the spine.

CUTTING EDGE   SCIENCE

Connecting images with lasers

For MRI scans to be useful during surgery, they have to be locked into precise alignment with live video images of the patient. This is achieved using a laser scanner. A laser is a device that makes a highly focused light beam. Laser beams are very narrow and can be controlled precisely. The laser scanner works by moving a beam of laser light rapidly backwards and forwards over the patient's head, measuring the distance from the scanner to the head at each point. The measurements are passed to a computer, which uses them to create a 'map' of the contours of the head. The computer also holds a detailed model of the patient's head built up by MRI scanning. It compares the contours of the laser map with the contours of the MRI model and rotates the model until it aligns exactly with the laser scan. Any changes in the position of the head are picked up by the laser scanner, and the MRI scan is moved in line with the head movements.

Opposite: An image of the type used by the surgeon shown on page 51 when carrying out brain surgery. The image shows the position of the brain tumour (yellow) that is the reason for the surgery, and major blood vessels around the tumour (purple).

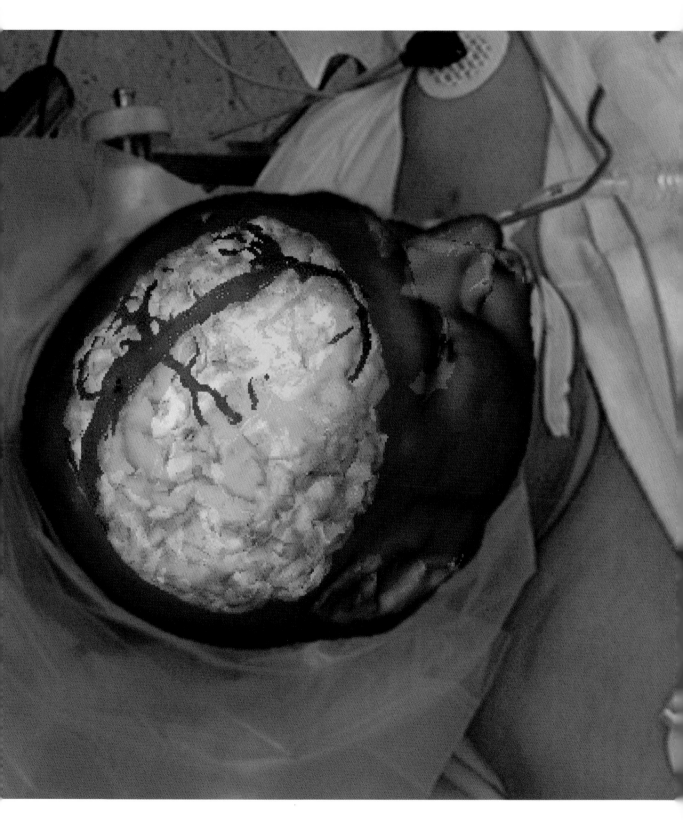

CHAPTER 11

Signposts to the Future

A man has been knocked down by a bus and is seriously injured. A passer-by calls an ambulance, which arrives within a few minutes. Although the victim does not have obvious injuries, he is in great pain. One of the ambulance crew uses a small magnetic device to switch off the pain centres in his brain. The other crew member pulls out a hand-held scanner and passes it over the patient's body. The scanner pinpoints the major areas of injury.

The ambulance crew send the images to the hospital. They are passed to the surgeon who will operate on the patient so that the surgeon can plan the operation. At the hospital, the surgeon repairs bleeding in the brain using keyhole surgery. She makes a small hole in the skull and inserts a tiny 'robot surgeon' which she operates by remote control. The robot stops the bleeding with a tiny laser.

The story above could not happen today – but it could occur in the near future. Medical imaging has made incredible strides since

CUTTING EDGE SCIENCE

TMS

TMS (transcranial magnetic stimulation) is a recently developed method for magnetically stimulating the brain. This may have potential as a treatment for depression. A pulse of magnetism from a TMS device can either stimulate part of the brain or briefly turn it off. TMS is being used in brain research, in combination with PET or fMRI imaging, to look at how brain activity is affected by magnetic stimulation. As well as its possible use in the treatment of depression, TMS might also be used to 'knock out' the pain centres of the brain for a short time to produce effective and safe pain relief.

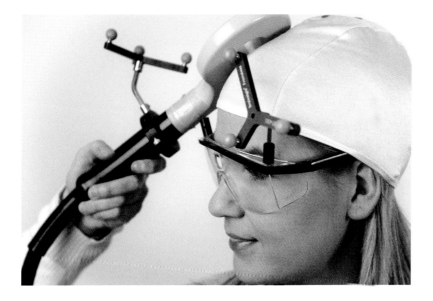

TMS equipment is being used here to map the brain. TMS is used to stimulate specific brain areas, and the effects of the stimulation on the patient are recorded. By stimulating different brain areas it is possible to build up a map of stimulation effects.

the first X-rays were made in 1896. But in the future the pace of change could be even faster. Thirty years from now, scanners will have changed beyond recognition.

Problems solved

Improvements to current scanners will soon be available. CT scanners that use two detectors with a single X-ray tube should scan twice as quickly as single-detector machines. The result will be better images with smaller doses of X-rays.

Open-sided MRI scanners are already in use, and new machines are being developed that can produce even better images. But an even more useful way of improving MRI scanners would be to make them smaller and cheaper. In 2004 two researchers working in the USA made important improvements to a very sensitive magnetic detector called an atomic magnetometer. The atomic magnetometer is far more sensitive than the detectors currently used in MRI scanners. A scanner with magnetometers as detectors would be much smaller, lighter and cheaper than current machines.

HUTT

Although existing scanners will continue to improve, a new kind of ultrasound scan known as high-resolution ultrasonic transmission tomography (HUTT) could prove itself superior to all the existing techniques. Conventional ultrasound scanners work by picking up the echoes of ultrasound pulses fired into the body. During an ultrasound scan, two thousand times as many sound waves pass through the body as bounce back as echoes. HUTT not only detects sound waves that pass through the body, but also detects how they have changed. HUTT scanners can therefore produce images with much greater resolution (clarity) and detail than conventional ultrasound scans – including those taken with the latest in 3-D technology. The images produced by HUTT scanning are even better than those obtainable from CT or MRI scanners.

As well as producing clear, detailed images, HUTT scanners can also differentiate between different kinds of body tissue. As the ultrasound passes through the body's tissues, they each change the ultrasound in different ways. Detectors can pick up these differences, and a computer can use the information to distinguish between the tissues.

Seeing with light

Another promising new imaging technique is optical imaging – scanning the body using light. Ordinary light does not pass through

CUTTING EDGE   SCIENCE

Seeing our thoughts?

In the future, will we be able to use imaging techniques to read people's thoughts? Using imaging combinations such as MRI and PET, scientists are already finding patterns of brain activity that may offer clues about what a person is thinking. As researchers obtain clearer images of these patterns and they get better at interpreting their meanings, it may become possible to read someone's thoughts from a brain scan. Some scientists are sceptical about this, however. They point to experiments that suggest there are no consistent patterns in brain activity and that people thinking similar things can show very different brain patterns.

the body. If it did, we would be transparent! However, some kinds of infrared light (radiation just below the red end of the light spectrum) are not absorbed by the body's tissues – they can pass right through the body. Researchers are now developing imaging

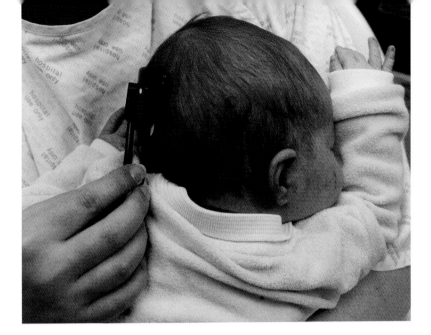

A hand-held optical imaging scanner is used to check a baby's brain. Optical imaging is useful here because babies are vulnerable to damage from X-rays, so CT scanning cannot be used. MRI is unsatisfactory because a baby cannot remain still for the time needed to do an MRI scan.

methods that shine infrared light though the body and then measure how the light is changed by its passage through the body. As with HUTT, it should be possible to use this information to build up images of the inside of the body.

Research carried out into the use of optical imaging for breast screening suggests that this technique could detect breast cancer earlier than any other imaging technique. Current optical imaging scanners can only penetrate about 15 centimetres beneath the skin. This is deep enough for breast screening, but it limits other uses of the technique.

Imaging in surgery

As medical imaging gains in speed, it will almost certainly become an essential part of surgery. Surgeons wearing virtual reality (VR) goggles will be able to see scans of the patient taken in real time, superimposed over video images of the patient's exterior. Through their VR goggles, surgeons will see markers indicating the exact positions of their surgical instruments as well as the area of the body they are targeting. As we saw in Chapter 10, much of this is already possible.

Tiny robots

Improvements in the camera pill described on pages 44 and 45 are set to revolutionize endoscopy. Instead of flexible tubes, doctors will introduce tiny robot cameras into the body. In 2004 a team of US researchers developed a robot camera about the size of an adult's thumb, which can be inserted into the abdomen. Once in place, the robot can be moved around by remote control. Robots like this could give a doctor 'eyes' inside a patient's body. Members of an ambulance crew at the scene of an accident could put a robot camera into a person's body, and doctors at the local hospital could look at the images and decide on the best emergency treatment for the patient. If sufficiently small robots are developed, it might even be possible to inject them into the bloodstream. Such robots could be used, for instance, to clear the kinds of blood clots that cause heart attacks and some kinds of stroke.

An exciting future

When X-rays were discovered, they caught the imagination of the whole world. For the first time we could look inside the living body without cutting it open. Today, images of the inside of the body are commonplace and of far higher quality than Wilhelm Röntgen could ever dream of. But the scanners that produce these pictures are large and expensive, and may soon be replaced by smaller, cheaper and more powerful models. The science of medical imaging is developing fast, and new, more sophisticated techniques for seeing inside the body are becoming available all the time. Hand-held scanners, micro-robots and virtual reality surgery are just some of the possibilities that could be in our hospitals in the not-too-distant future.

An artist's impression of microscopic medical robots at work in the human body. We may soon be able to make devices that can travel through blood vessels and other parts of the body. One type could carry a camera and other medical imaging equipment. Another could carry tiny surgical tools or drugs to treat any problems they find.

CUTTING EDGE   FACTS

Milestones in medical imaging

Date	Event
1895	Wilhelm Röntgen discovers X-rays.
1896	Thomas Edison demonstrates the fluoroscope.
1904	Clarence Dally, Edison's assistant, dies from X-ray burns.
1910	Hans Christian Jacobeus uses a rigid endoscope to look inside the chest.
1913	The Bucky grid and the Coolidge tube greatly improve X-ray quality.
1921	Jan Sicard and Jacques Forestier first use lipidiol as a contrast medium.
1928	S. Y. Sokolov makes the first ultrasound fault detector.
1931	International agreement is reached on a maximum safe X-ray dose.
1934	George Hevesy uses the first radioactive tracer.
1937	Karl and Friedrich Dussik obtain crude ultrasound images of the brain.
1946	Edward Purcell and Felix Bloch develop NMR.
1949–51	Early ultrasound research is conducted in the USA.
1955	The image intensifier makes it possible to look at X-rays on a TV screen.
1957	Basil Hirschowitz and colleagues develop the first flexible endoscope.
1959	Ian Donald first uses ultrasound on pregnant women.
1968	The first SPECT machines are introduced.
1970–77	Early work is carried out on MRI by Raymond Damadian and Paul Lauterbur.
1971	The first CT scanner is demonstrated by Godfrey Hounsfield.
1975	The first PET machines are built. Improved ultrasound machines become widespread.
1977	Damadian demonstrates the first whole-body MRI scanner.
Early 1980s	The first commercial MRI scanners become available.
1990	Seiji Ogawa and colleagues demonstrate fMRI.
2001	Commercial 3-D ultrasound machines become available. The first camera pill is developed.
2005	The first demonstrations of HUTT.

Glossary

abdomen The stomach area of the body.

Alzheimer's disease A brain disorder that causes older people to progressively lose their memory and their ability to write or even speak.

angiography The process of taking X-ray images of the blood vessels by injecting a contrast medium (a liquid that X-rays cannot pass through) into the bloodstream.

arteriosclerosis A condition in which the walls of the arteries (blood vessels carrying blood from the heart to the rest of the body) thicken and harden.

atoms The fundamental particles from which all substances are composed.

bronchoscope A type of endoscope that is used to examine the lungs.

cancer An illness in which a group or groups of cells begin to grow uncontrollably.

cartilage A strong, springy kind of tissue that forms some parts of the skeleton and of joints.

catheter A thin, flexible tube that can be inserted into a blood vessel or other part of the body to inject or drain off fluids.

cathode ray tube A glass tube with the air pumped out of it, containing two electrodes that allow electricity to be passed through the tube.

colon The lower part of the digestive tract.

cyclotron A large machine used for studying atoms and subatomic particles. Radioisotopes are also made in cyclotrons.

cyst An abnormal sac that develops inside the body, which may be filled with fluid or fibrous material.

diagnosis The identifying of an illness or disorder in a patient.

electromagnetic radiation The different wavelengths of mostly invisible energy waves (radiation) that travel at the speed of light; includes visible light, X-rays, radio waves, microwaves, infrared (heat) radiation and gamma rays.

endoscope A thin, often flexible tube with a lens at one end, which is used to look inside the body.

endoscopy The practice of looking into the body and/or performing surgery using an endoscope.

epilepsy A disorder of the nervous system in which the patient sometimes has bouts of uncontrollable movements or unconsciousness.

fetus A developing unborn child more than eight weeks old.

fluorescent A material that glows when light or some other kind of radiation hits it.

gamma rays Very high-energy electromagnetic radiation produced by some radioactive substances.

Geiger counter An instrument for detecting and measuring radioactivity.

glucose A sugar that is the main fuel used by cells to produce the energy they need to work and grow.

HUTT High-resolution ultrasonic transmission tomography – a type of ultrasound scanner that detects how sound waves change as they pass through the body, thereby producing images of exceptional detail and clarity.

incision A cut made by a surgeon during an operation.

inflammation A swelling of a joint or other body part.

intestine The long tube that forms the part of the digestive system beyond the stomach.

keyhole surgery Surgery performed through small incisions in the body, using endoscopes.

laparoscopy The use of an endoscope to look at and/or perform surgery on the abdomen or pelvic area (lower part of the body).

laser A device that produces a highly focused, pure beam of light.

leukaemia A kind of cancer that affects the white blood cells.

multiple sclerosis A disease that causes gradual, worsening damage to the nervous system.

optical fibres Flexible fibres made from glass that conduct light along their length.

organ A part of the body with a particular function, such as the heart, the liver or the stomach.

pacemaker An electrical device inserted in the chest, which helps the heart to beat in a normal rhythm.

paralysed Unable to move all or part of the body.

pituitary gland A small organ in the brain that produces chemicals that circulate in the blood and control the actions of hormones in the body.

positron An incredibly small particle, similar to an electron, but with a positive electric charge. An electron is an extremely small particle with a negative electric charge, which forms part of an atom.

radiation Waves or rays of energy, such as light, X-rays, radio waves and infrared.

radioactive Describes a substance that emits (gives out) radiation.

radioisotope A form of an element that is radioactive.

radiology The science of X-rays and other kinds of high-energy radiation.

telesurgery Surgery in which the surgeon operates on the patient from a distance, using remote control.

tissue A part of the body made from cells that are all similar. Muscle, bone and skin are types of tissue.

tomography The technique of making images of slices through the body.

tumour An abnormal growth in the body. Some tumours are benign – they stop growing after a short time and stay in one place. Others are malignant – they invade surrounding tissues and spread to other organs.

ulcer A sore patch in the body caused by a break in the skin or a membrane.

ultrasound Very high-pitched sounds, beyond the range of human hearing.

vacuum Completely empty space, without air or other gases in it.

voxels Small blocks that make up a 3-D computer image. Voxels are similar to the pixels (the individual tiny dots) that make up a flat computer image.

Further Information

BOOKS

History of Medicine: Medicine In the Twentieth Century by Alex Woolf (Hodder Wayland, 2006)

Horrible Science: Bulging Brains by Nick Arnold (Scholastic Hippo, 1999)

Inventors and Inventions: Radiology by by K. Winkler (Cherrytree Books, 1998)

The Mysterious Rays of Dr Roentgen by Beverley Gherman (Atheneum Books for Young Readers, 1994)

Naked to the Bone by Bettyann Holzmann Kevles (Basic Books, 1997)

Technology All Around Us: Medicine by Kristina Routh (Franklin Watts, 2005)

WEBSITES

imaginis.com/faq/history.asp
This website has an overview of the history of medical imaging, including a timeline of milestones in medical imaging, and links to other useful material.

www.xray.hmc.psu.edu/rci/centennial.html
A website on the history of X-rays since their discovery in 1895. The text is more suitable for older readers, but the website includes many interesting historical photographs.

nobelprize.org/medicine/laureates/1979/hounsfield-autobio.html
An autobiography of Godfrey Hounsfield, the man who invented CT, from the Nobel Prize website.

imagers.gsfc.nasa.gov/ems/ems.html
An explanation of electromagnetic radiation and the electromagnetic spectrum.

Index

Index *(continued)*